Shopping Addiction Therapy

Stop The Credit Card Abuse - Addiction Treatment For Shopping Addicts

Table of Contents

Introduction

I want to thank you and congratulate you for purchasing the book, *"Shopping Addiction Therapy: Stop The Credit Card Abuse - Addiction Treatment For Shopping Addicts"*.

This book contains proven steps and strategies for how to better understand your addiction to shopping so you can start taking steps to build a better future for you and your family. No matter what your situation is right now, you can still create an abundant, happy and fulfilling life. You just need to realize that you are in control and you can do something about your situation. Through this book, you will learn different tools that you can use to recover from your shopping addiction and to start living the life you want for yourself and family.

Thanks again for purchasing this book, I hope you enjoy it!

Chapter 1: What Is Shopping Addiction?

Shopping has become a favorite pastime of many Americans, especially during weekends, paydays and holidays. Some people can become satisfied by shopping for small trinkets or knick knacks for the house, while others feel that they need to shop for new clothes and shoes regularly to relieve their stress from day-to-day life. This is where the danger lies, because a regular pastime can develop into a genuine and vicious addiction that can destroy not only your finances, but the other areas of your life, as well.

According to Dr. Donald Black who is a professor teaching psychiatry at the University of Iowa, "Compulsive shopping and spending are defined as inappropriate, excessive and out of control. Like other addictions, it basically has to do with impulsiveness and lack of control over one's impulses. In America, shopping is embedded in our culture, so often, the impulsiveness comes out as excessive shopping."

Shopping addiction is sometimes called compulsive buying or "shopoholism" and a lot of people's lives have been destroyed by it. If you think you have this addiction, it is recommended that you learn more about it so you can better understand how excessive shopping can become addictive and how you can stop yourself from getting deeper into the addiction.

According to Ruth Engs, a professor teaching applied health science at the Indiana University, "No one knows what causes addictive behaviors, like shopping, alcoholism, drug abuse and gambling. Some of the new evidence suggests that some people, maybe 10%-15% may have a genetic predisposition to an addictive behavior coupled with an environment in which the particular behavior is triggered, but no one really knows why."

But even though the cause of addictive behaviors is still undefined, there is now better understanding on why addicts carry on with their harmful behaviors despite the damage inflicted in their lives. Ruth Engs further explained that when people start getting some sort of high from their addictions, their dopamine and endorphin levels are increased which makes them feel better. Our brains naturally produce both hormones and they make us do the things that make us feel better more often. They actually reinforce addictive behaviors. This is why it is important for you to watch out for telltale signs to ensure that your shopping sprees do not become a shopping addiction.

What is shopoholism?

According to Ruth Engs, shopaholics and other addicts share a lot of common behaviors. For example, alcoholics normally hide their alcohol bottles from their loved ones, while shopaholics hide their shopping bags and other evidences of shopping from their family and friends. Here are some of the other indications that you may have crossed the line towards shopping addiction:

- Splurging over budget. Your shopping hobby can already be considered an addiction when you constantly spend more than your budget or even your income. Normal people will think twice before buying something that they cannot really afford. But a shopping addict will not waste even a second to consider the consequences. If you are starting to experience financial troubles because of your spending habit, you may need to consider seeking some help.

- Compulsive buying. How many times have you planned to go to the mall to just buy one essential item and end up buying new clothes and shoes that you do not really need?

- Persistent issue. Almost everyone goes out on shopping sprees during holiday seasons and on 2 to 3 other special occasions every year. If you notice that your unmanageable shopping sprees happen more than these instances, you may have an addiction to shopping.

- Hiding the issue. Do you leave your shopping bags in the trunk of your car because you do not want your spouse or partner to see them and criticize your spending? Do you have a credit card account that you keep secret from your spouse? Shopping addiction is more common in women, just as alcoholism is more common in men. A lot of husbands have reported that they are surprised when they learned that their wives are deep in credit card debt and that they are obligated to pay off tens of thousands of debts from their wives' shopping sprees. These instances normally result to a divorce.

- Shopping in a vicious cycle. A shopping addict feels guilty after a big shopping splurge. Because they feel guilty, they are then triggered to go on another shopping spree to relieve the tension. This can then go on and on in a vicious cycle. You may not really get into credit card debt if you constantly return clothes when you are feeling guilty, but you know that a serious issue still exists and you need to deal with it.

- Damaged relationships. Your excessive shopping or compulsive buying can actually impair your personal and work relationships. When you spend a lot of time shopping instead of attending to your family, you not only fail to create strong relationships, but you also destroy whatever relationships you have created before. Your spouse starts to become suspicious of your every move because he or she has caught you lying about your shopping sprees. You start to isolate yourself physically and emotionally because of your preoccupation with shopping and because of the guilt you feel afterwards.

- Obvious consequences. Shopping addiction is really like all other kinds of addiction. It is not really about how much money you spend or how much time you waste shopping. It is all about the consequences of your actions. Now, if I ask you, when someone spends more money than they has planned to spend during holiday shopping, would you consider them to be a shopping addict? You are correct when you answer no. But when your shopping splurges starts to follow a trend or pattern and you constantly find yourself dealing with negative consequences of your compulsive buying, you may already be considered to be a shopping addict. When you feel like you cannot control your shopping habit and you cannot stop yourself from spending more when you know that you will face a negative consequence, it's time to seek help.

Here are other negative behaviors that can indicate that you might have a shopping addiction:

- You go on a shopping splurge when you cannot deal with your negative emotions, such as loneliness, anger, depression and anxiety.

- You catch yourself having frequent arguments with other people because of your spending habits.

- You feel lost when your credit cards are not with you. You feel withdrawal symptoms when you go out of the house without them.

- You always purchase items using your credit card instead of cash.

- You can actually feel a sense of euphoria or rush when you are out shopping.

- After a big shopping spree, you feel guilt, shame and embarrassment.

- You lie to other people about the amount of money you spend. You may actually own up to purchasing something, but you still lie about its actual cost.

- You catch yourself obsessively thinking about money.

- You spend a lot of time managing your bills and bank accounts in order to accommodate your shopping sprees.

If you think you have at least four of the above behaviors, you may be actually addicted to shopping and now is the best time to seek help.

Chapter 2: Seeking Help For Your Shopping Addiction

According to an article published in World Psychiatry, around 6 percent of Americans face compulsive shopping issues at least once in their lives. The percentage is even higher when other methods of study were used. As mentioned in the previous chapter, shopping addicts are very similar to other addicts because they will go to great lengths in order to conceal their purchases and shopping activities. A lot of people refuse to confront their compulsive buying problems until they are deep in credit card debts and have reached "rock bottom". They continue with their destructive behaviors despite the severe financial outcomes. They lose more than just money and other material possessions. They also lose the trust of their family and even their career.

But even if you are at your own "rock bottom" now, always believe that there is hope for you. You can recover from your shopping addiction and live a fulfilling, abundant and happy life. You just need to be willing to take the first step, which is to admit that you indeed have shopping issues. Only after you have taken this crucial step will you become motivated to seek further help.

There are no standard treatments for shopping addiction. But experts use two primary forms of therapy: Cognitive-Behavioral Therapy or CBT and medication. Several clinical studies have been conducted to assess the effectiveness of medication treatments for shopping addiction. The studies involved medications that are usually prescribed for depression and anxiety patients. The results are mixed and there are several medical experts who are not keen on prescribing medications to treat shopping addiction.

More medical experts are partial to prescribing Cognitive-Behavioral Therapy. CBT is generally used to describe the method used to identify and correct issues linked to how we think, act and feel. Your thoughts, actions and emotions all contribute to your compulsive or addictive behaviors.

Cognitive-Behavioral Therapy focuses on the issues that arise from within you instead of from influences from the outside. It can help you through spending quality time with mental health experts, your family and friends in situations related to your problem, where you can reorganize and reform your emotions, thoughts and history. There are several options that you can choose from:

- Guided cognitive-behavioral therapy, where a mental health expert (counselor, therapist or psychologist) aids you in your recovery process.

- Self-help CBT, where you read self-books and other reading materials and keep a shopping journal.

- Charity or volunteer CBT programs, where you obtain support while you take practical steps in curbing your urges to shop. You can visit the Debtors Anonymous website to learn more.

Many experts advise their patients to combine the above options so they can come up with a treatment program that is suitable to their personal needs. You may also need to address the issues in the other areas of your life that have suffered from your shopping addiction. You and your spouse may consider undergoing marriage counseling to restore your relationship. You can also opt to have financial counseling to help you recover from your debts and other financial losses.

You need to change your spending habits.

You need to realize that for you to recover from your shopping addiction, you will need to change a lot of your spending habits. You will never be able to completely eliminate all the temptations that can trigger your compulsion to buy. You need to take certain actions that can help you resist those temptations and control how you spend your hard earned money. Since all addictions involve a lack of self-control, you need to start developing your self-control so you can become stronger than your urges. You can opt to start a regular fitness regime, a healthier food diet or other activities that require self-control or self-discipline. You will realize that the rewards for your efforts will be worthwhile.

It is also wrong to totally ban shopping for the rest of your life. A lot of people have referred to shopping as "retail therapy" because it can really help people relax and delight in the fruits of their hard work. You can still go out and shop. You just need to help yourself to rediscover the pleasure of healthy shopping. You need to create a plan that can aid in getting you back in control of your life. You need to create new and good shopping habits so you will not fall for your old, bad ones. As you substitute a bad habit with a good one, you make yourself stronger in controlling your shopping urges.

Here are useful tips that can aid you during your recovery from shopping addiction:

- Understand your shopping addiction. Stop hiding or lying about your shopping activities and purchases. Instead, try to understand yourself and your shopping addiction more. What triggers you to go on shopping sprees? Write down the money concerns that you have been worrying about obsessively. Write down your debts and create a plan for how you can repay them. Arm yourself with information so that you can face your shopping problems head on.

- Know yourself. You need to dig deep inside you to understand your cravings to buy and buy. Does the excitement of hunting for good bargains thrill you? Do you always want to be ahead of your friends when it comes to fashion or gadgets? Do you have a weakness for certain kinds of items like gadgets, clothing or shoes? Saying, "Yes" to these questions does not essentially mean that you have a shopping problem. But it is always ideal to examine yourself so you can prevent yourself from crossing the line.

- Ponder how you feel every time you go out and shop. Observe any emotional triggers that normally cause you to go on a shopping spree. Do you find yourself buying unnecessary things when you are feeling anxious, depressed, lonely or angry? Do you use shopping as an excuse to cheer you up after a long day? When you understand your emotions better, you can better focus on the right methods of coping with your feelings.

- Consider the amount of time you waste on shopping. Do you have projects that remain unfinished because you are always out shopping? Do you fail to spend quality time with your family and friends because you are always busy juggling your finances and surfing online deals? One effective way to conquer your shopping addiction is to commit to spend more time doing more valuable things than wasting it in shopping for unnecessary things.

- • Be in control of your situation. Instead of feeling helpless because of the negative consequences of your shopping addiction, keep in mind that you can still control your own life. Do not try to solve all your problems all at once. Take it one step at a time. Start with the things that you can actually control. This is a good time to get rid of your credit cards so you can start paying for your purchases with checks, debit cards or cash. Refuse all offers for unsecured debt. Stop adding to your problems and take small steps to reduce your existing debts. Change your lifestyle. Sell everything that you do not really need and use the money to pay off your debts.

- Keep a journal of your expenses. Writing down all of your expenses on a day-to-day basis can help you realize how much money you are spending. It is also ideal to summarize your daily expenses at the end of the month so you can see where your money goes to and see where you can cut back. It is even better if you can come up with a budget that you can use to limit your purchases and expenditures.

- Stay away from non-essential temptations. Admitting that you have a shopping problem can help you to avoid shopping districts, malls and discount warehouses. If it is impossible for you to completely avoid these shopping places, so make sure that you regularly create a shopping list that you can stick to. Stop yourself from window-shopping unless the stores are already closed. Throw away store catalogues as soon as you get them. Unsubscribe from the online newsletters of online stores. Stop watching shopping channels on television. If you truly need to shop at a place that is particularly irresistible for you, take along a reliable friend who understands your shopping issues and can firmly tell you to abide by your shopping list.

- Look for healthy alternatives to shopping. Find other activities that can give you the same good feelings that you can get from shopping. You can try going out for a walk in the park. You can bike or do yoga. You can learn a new hobby that you have always wanted to try. Look for things that can divert your attention when the urge to splurge is great.

- Expand your possibilities. Rather than wasting a lot of your time shopping, you can opt to spend more quality time with your family and friends. You can also volunteer your time helping other people. If you need to lose weight, focus on that. Read books. You can even take new classes.

- Know when you need to seek help. There will be times when it will be particularly difficult for you to control your urge to shop. These are the times when you just can't fight your battle alone. You will need to ask for help from your family and friends. If you need to, seek out therapy or counseling. You can also opt to regularly attend a Debtors Anonymous meeting to connect with other people who are going through the same struggles. Simply visit the website of Debtors Anonymous to look for a meeting in your local area.

Chapter 3: Get Out Of Debt

One of the first steps you need to take to reclaim your financial future after shopping addiction is to pay off all your debts. No matter how deep in debt you may be, always remember that there is hope for you. Here are some steps that can make it easier for you:

- Do not delay action. Just as interest on investments are compounded over time, the interest on some of your debts can also escalate if you delay paying them off.

- Start creating your get-out-of-debt strategy. You can do this by listing down all your debts per creditor. Include the existing amount that you owe, the corresponding interest rate and the required minimum payments that you need to pay every month. It is better to use a computer worksheet such as MS Excel so you can sort your debts according interest rate (from highest to lowest). Plan your payment strategy in such a way that you can pay as much as you can on debts with the highest interest rates while making the minimum payments on your other financial obligations. This way, you will not have to pay the high interest rates for a long time and use the money to pay off the principal amounts of your debts. Even better, if you can, pay more than the minimum amounts every month. Every time you are able to eliminate one debt, celebrate your progress. Make sure that you do not add new debts to the list.

- One you have paid off one of your debts, use the monthly payment you have allotted for it to pay off the next debt with the highest interest rate.

- Cut back on your expenditures. You can do this more easily by recording your actual day-to-day expenditures and disbursements. Then at the end of the month, summarize your expenses and see which items you can cut back on. Here are some smart buying tips which can help you lessen your expenses:

  - ✓ Make it a priority to purchase the things that you truly need. Then you can proceed to buying a couple of reasonably priced "wants".

  - ✓ Instead of going to department stores and big-box stores to shop, opt to go to flea markets, thrift stores, garage sales, consignment stores and outlet stores. Always try to negotiate for lower prices.

  - ✓ Stick to the basic services for your phone, Internet and cable TV subscriptions. Do not subscribe to expensive add-on services that you can do without.

  - ✓ Purchase clothes in classic styles instead of trendy styles that can easily go out of fashion. Do not sacrifice high-quality fabrics over price. They last longer and you can save more money in the long run.

✓ Create your shopping list before going out to shop. Make sure that you stick to your list to avoid impulse buying.

✓ Do not purchase food items from expensive convenience stores. Plan for your meals so you can take advantage of bulk discounts from food warehouses and supermarkets.

✓ Consider buying store brands at drugstores and supermarkets when available. A lot of these store brands have the same quality when compared to name brands without costing as much.

✓ You may also use coupons to get discounts. But make sure that you check first if buying a name brand with a coupon is indeed cheaper than buying the same item in store brand.

✓ Purchase items that you regularly use in bulk. Be on the lookout for discounts on these items and stock up. You just need to ensure that you are not buying more than you will reasonably use. Also check the expiration dates of the items to make sure that they will not spoil before you can actually use them.

✓ Instead of dining out which can really be expensive, cook simple but delicious meals at home. Bring your own lunch to work. You will not only be able to save money but you can also eat healthier foods.

- ✓ Use public transportation as often as possible. Look for people who you can share driving with.

- ✓ Every couple of years, canvass for the best rates on car insurance.

- ✓ Talk with your relatives, friends and neighbors to see if you can trade baby-sitting with them.

- ✓ Instead of buying new books, CDs and DVDs, go to your local library to borrow them for free. Cut your newspaper and magazine subscriptions. You can always read the news online or from your local library.

- ✓ Make sure that you are staying within the texting and call limits of your cell phone service to avoiding paying extra.

- ✓ Instead of paying for long-distance calls and posts, try using free online apps such as Skype and Facebook Messenger.

- ✓ Explore your creativity and give gifts that you made yourself.

- ✓ Instead of paying for repair services, perform the simple repair works around your home yourself.

- Sell your stuff that you rarely use. It is ideal to sell them yourself instead of getting an

Internet broker or bringing them to a pawnshop.

- Be honest in assessing your capability to pay for something and then do the correct action. For instance, you purchased a new car and you found yourself having troubles in paying the monthly mortgage. It is a lot better to sell the car and paying off the remaining balance of your car loan and then buying a new car with lesser cost or even a second-hand car that suits your budget. If you choose not to be practical about your situation, you run the risk of eventually losing the car to the bank when you cannot repay your car loan.

- Look for ways to increase your income. You can get another job if your schedule can accommodate it. You can also talk to your supervisor or boss to see if it is possible for you to do some overtime work. Whatever extra income you earn, make sure that you use it to pay off your debts. But you also need to make sure that any extra time you spend working will not affect your family life. You should never neglect your spouse and children just so you can earn more to pay off your debts.

- Talk to your creditors to see if you can apply for a loan consolidation. You can stop incurring more interest charges by consolidating your high interest loans into one loan that has a lower interest rate.

- Throw away your numerous credit cards except a couple for emergency purposes. Make sure to contact the credit card companies so they will cancel your accounts and stop further charges. Do not bring your emergency credit cards with you when you go out and shop. You can also opt to request for a lower credit limit to avoid incurring huge debts. But you also need to know that your credit score may be affected when you cancel your credit card accounts. It is important to strike a balance between eliminating your debts and maintaining or improving your credit score.

- You can contact 1-888-5OPTOUT (1-888-567-8688) to prevent new credit card offers from being sent to your mail. You can get further information from www.optoutpreescreen.com.

Choose bankruptcy as your last resort.

As much as possible, try to get out of debt without declaring bankruptcy, because it can affect everyone. Actually, an average household in the U.S. will have to incur an additional $400 for every bankruptcy declared. This is because businesses charge higher prices every time their customers declare bankruptcy.

It is also wrong to believe that bankruptcy is a "quick fix" that can eliminate all of your debt problems. Yes, it can reduce most of your debts but it cannot eliminate all of your debts, particularly child support and taxes. Yes, you can finally say goodbye to collection agencies who kept harassing you, but you will have to face far more serious consequences on your life in the future.

To get a better grasp on the effects of bankruptcy, it is good to understand that two kinds of bankruptcy are available to you as a consumer:

Chapter 7 Bankruptcy

After declaring a Chapter 7 bankruptcy, your assets will be sold and whatever proceeds will be used to pay off your debts. You will not actually be required to sell all of your assets. You can still keep some of your personal properties including your car, but you may still lose some of your most valued possessions. Filing for Chapter 7 Bankruptcy will not also eliminate some of your debts, including child support, alimony, taxes and student loans. Recently several other kinds of debts have been included in the list of debts not eliminated by a Chapter 7 bankruptcy. This means that your credit score will still reflect them for as long as ten years.

In 2005, there were several changes made to the federal bankruptcy laws that made it harder for a lot of people to qualify for Chapter 7. For instance, an applicant does not only need to first meet the eligibility requirements under a "means test", but must accomplish compulsory credit counseling from a government accredited program as well. Because of these stricter changes, more people have been compelled to apply for a Chapter 13 bankruptcy instead.

Chapter 13 Bankruptcy

This type of bankruptcy is basically a scheme to pay off all your outstanding debts. You will be required to make your installments payments directly to the court and then a trustee will forward your payments to your creditors. Generally, most creditors settle for a lesser payment amount instead of getting nothing from their debtors. You will be able to keep all of your assets as long as you are able to promptly pay your monthly dues. You need to note that your Chapter 13 bankruptcy will be reflected in your credit report for a minimum of 7 years.

Seeking Help in Paying Off Your Debts

You do not need to go through your struggle alone. Help is available for you. Here are some ways you can seek help and support from other people:

- Even before you start missing your monthly payments, contact your creditors to discuss different alternatives. This can really be a tough step to take but just think that it is a lot less distressing than receiving phone calls from collectors who demand payment from you. Usually, creditors are willing to work with their debtors to come up with a workable payment plan. Some options include dividing your outstanding balance into smaller payment amounts or even waiving some of your interest charges or principal amount. Take courage and negotiate with your creditors. Just make sure that all of your agreed terms are in writing so that you will have proof to present in case there is confusion in the future.

- Seek help from the National Foundation for Credit Counseling (1-800-388-2227 or www.nfcc.org) or other not-for-profit credit counseling services. These organizations can help you in creating a budget and negotiating with your creditors.

- Avoid availing of the services of "credit repair" organizations that claim that they can fix your credit history. No one else but you can repair your bad credit history. You can only do this by paying off all your outstanding debts and meeting your current dues on time. Do not believe such claims as "We can eliminate your bad credit with 100% guarantee". They are absolutely not true.

Learn How to Use Your Credit Card Wisely

The interest charges on your outstanding credit card balances are not really cheap. Furthermore, credit cards can make it very easy for you to get deep in debt. But I am not really saying that you should stop using a credit card altogether. If we think about it, a credit card is a more convenient and safer means of paying compared to cash. If ever your credit card is stolen or got lost, you will only be responsible for unauthorized charges below $50. The credit card company will refund any unauthorized charges above that amount, as long as you immediately report your missing credit card.

There are also certain situations when a credit card is necessary. In order for you to make certain kinds of purchases, you need to use either a debit card or credit card. This includes online purchases, airline tickets, hotel reservations and car rentals. It is also good to have a credit card to pay for unexpected expenses like car repairs, especially when you have not yet set up a sizeable emergency fund.

You can also enhance your credit score by using your credit card wisely. Your credit score can increase as you use your credit card to pay for your purchases and to pay for your outstanding balances promptly. This means that you should only use your credit card for transactions that you are certain you have funds to pay for. You also need to keep in mind that interest rates increase as your credit score decreases. Taking care of your credit rating can indeed benefit you in the long term.

Chapter 4: Start A Savings Habit

Aside from paying off your debts, your financial goals should include creating robust savings habits. Every time you save money, it is just like you are saying, "I am looking forward to a good future for myself and my family and I am willing to be responsible for it". When you save, you are showing that you have faith in yourself and in your future. Do not worry if you think that you have always failed in setting up a savings plan before. There is still hope for you. I hope that this chapter can help you.

Starting to save early really pays.

Those who save earlier in life have a bigger advantage when compared to those who started at a later time. The reason for this is really basic. Every time you save even a small amount of money, you are activating the principle of the time value of money. The principal amount of your savings earns interest income, which in turn has the capability of increasing your income further if added back to your original principal. This process is referred to as "compounding" and its benefits can be greatly experienced over time.

Commit to save today.

Your commitment is actually the first step to successful saving. You need to believe that you deserve to live an abundant, happy and fulfilling life and you can do something to make that a reality. Do not believe other people who discourage you by saying that it is impossible or hard to do. Even if you barely make ends meet and your family is living on a hand to mouth or paycheck-to-paycheck basis, you can still create a workable savings plan. You just need to always keep in mind that savings is just one of your necessities.

I want to share with you the most fundamental and important principle in saving: always pay yourself first. After you have received your paycheck, you need to commit to paying yourself (through savings) first before paying your bills and other expenses. Instead of working with the "income – expenses = savings" formula, work with the "income – savings = expenses" formula. When you work with the first formula, you may always find yourself not having anything set aside for your savings account. You need to discipline yourself and your family to live with whatever is available after you have set aside the money for your savings account.

If you are getting anxious now because you still think it is impossible to start saving today, read these practical techniques that can help you:

- Talk to your employer to see if it is possible to set up an automatic deduction from your regular paycheck that will go directly to your savings account. This way, you can treat your savings just like any of the mandatory deductions you have at work. Don't worry. You do not really need to start big. As small as $20 to $50 per month can go a long way, as long as you are consistent with your savings.

- You can also talk to your bank to request for an automatic transfer from your checking account to your savings account every payday. This basically works like the first option.

- You can put $1 (or more) into a jar. By the end of the month, you will have around $30 in your jar, which you can then deposit into your savings account. This is actually an easy way for you to train your subconscious about how simple saving really is. A dollar a day seems negligible but it can really go a long way over time.

- Instead of going straight to the mall after receiving a bonus, pay raise or tax refund, commit to depositing a huge chunk of the money to your savings account.

- When planning your monthly budget, make sure that savings is included as part of your regular "expenses". Commit to prioritize your savings over other expenses such as dining out and going to the movies.

- Submit product rebates. After you have received the check for the rebates, immediately deposit it into your savings account.

Where to Put Your Pay and Your Savings

You might have correctly deduced by now that you will need to open a savings account in order for you to successfully create your savings fund. But aside from a savings account, you will also need a checking account where you can deposit your paychecks. A checking account is a very convenient, safe and economical method of paying your bills. You can open both your savings and checking accounts from any bank, savings, credit union and loan association. It can be more convenient to open both your checking and savings accounts at the same bank, but this is not really required. But you can inquire with your bank to see if they will give you a free checking account if you also open a savings account with them. Always double check the terms and agreement that you are entering in to when opening a checking account to make sure that you understand the corresponding charges and fees for the transactions. Unlike a savings account that earns you interest income when you let your money stay on deposit, a checking account does not pay you any form of income.

What to Look for in a Checking Account

It is always ideal to compare the different checking accounts available from different banks and financial institutions to see which one is the most beneficial for you. You can use the following questions in making your assessment:

- What is the minimum initial deposit requirement?

- What is the minimum balance required so I will not be charged with any fees?

- What fees will be charged to my checking account on a regular basis?

- Are there additional benefits if I maintain a higher balance in my account?

- Will I be charged every time I write a check?

- How much is the cost of a new check?

- Do you have a "basic" checking account with lower charges and fees if I only use a couple of checks every month?

- Do you offer a checking account that earns interest? If yes, what are the minimum initial deposit and the minimum maintaining balance?

- How much are the penalties for maintaining balance below minimum, "non-sufficient funds or NSF" and bounced checks?

- Do you offer an overdraft protection?

- Are there extra fees when I use the ATM?

- Are there extra fees if I transact with your bank teller?

- For banks, are you insured by the FDIC or the Federal Deposit Insurance Corporation?

- For credit unions, are you insured by the NCUA or the National Credit Union Administration?

How to Make the Most Out of Your Checking Account

Aside from being a convenient mode of payment, checking accounts have new features that can help you manage your finances more conveniently. For instance, you can request your employer to have your salary be directly credited (through funds transfer) into your checking account. This way, your salary will be immediately available on your account on payday, which you can readily use. You no longer need to go out of your way to go to the bank and spend a long time waiting in line to access your funds. You also have lesser risk of having your paycheck stolen or losing/misplacing it. Most banks also currently offer online banking wherein you can readily check the balance of your account and the transactions that have been debited or credited. This makes it a lot easier for you to track your funds.

Automatic bills payment is another common feature of many checking accounts. You can set up recurring payments for your bills such as mortgage payments or car loan payments so that the payable amount can be directly transferred from your checking account to the bank account of your creditors. Aside from eliminating the risk of you forgetting to pay your bills and paying late charges, you can also save time and money since you do not need to write and mail checks every month. But if you plan to do automatic bills payment, you need to make sure that you are regularly tracking the balance of your checking account to make sure that there are always enough funds to cover your automatic payments. Do not allow your checking account to be overdrawn to avoid paying extra charges, which could actually be costly.

Here are some useful tips that can help you ensure that you have full control of your checking account:

- Make it a habit to always keep track of your account balance. You can opt to manually write down your transactions in the checkbook register or you can simply enroll your account in online banking so you can check your balance anytime and anywhere, as long as you have access to the Internet.

- If you prefer to manually track your balance, ensure that you record all transactions, including any withdrawals you make from the ATM and charges you make using your debit card.

- Do not ever write a check for an amount that is not available in your checking account. You will not only run the risk of paying expensive NSF or non-sufficient funds penalty charges, which can be as costly as $35, for every check that bounced, but your credit rating can also be negatively affected. The business party you are transacting with may also charge you with penalty charges for every bounced payment that you make.

- Using a debit card can also be tricky. Avoid using a debit card when the balance in your checking account is running low. There are some businesses that approve a transaction amount that is higher than what is actually available in your account. When this happens, you will be charged for overdrawing your checking account.

- One good reason why you should manually track your checking account balance is that you can use your records to compare the transactions reflected in the bank statement forwarded to you every month. It is ideal to perform reconciliation between your records and the bank's figures so that you can catch any transactions that you have not authorized such as double posting of payments. When you see any discrepancies, immediately contact your bank so that they can refund whatever erroneous transaction has been charged to your account.

What to Look For in a Savings Account

There are a lot of banks and financial institutions that offer savings accounts. It is a good idea to look around first before deciding to open a savings account, so you can see which one best fits your requirements. You can use the following questions in making your assessment:

- What is the minimum initial deposit requirement?

- What is the minimum balance required so I will not be charged with any fees?

- How much interest will my money earn?

- How frequent will my account be credited with the interest I earned?

- What are my options when I want to withdraw money from my account?

- Are there limitations to the frequency of withdrawals from my account every month so that I do not incur any charges? (Always keep in mind that you need to avoid charges because your objective in opening a savings account is to save money and earn interest along the way.)

- Will the interest rate be affected when I withdraw money from my savings account?

- Are there extra fees when I use the ATM?

- Are there extra fees if I transact with your bank teller?

- For banks, are you insured by the FDIC or the Federal Deposit Insurance Corporation?

- For credit unions, are you insured by the NCUA or the National Credit Union Administration?

Aside from a savings account, you may also consider saving your money in a Money Market Deposit Account or in Certificates of Deposit (CD's), where you can normally earn more interest compared to a standard savings account. But because you will be earning more from these investment vehicles, you will have to do some trade-offs. With CD's, you will be required to keep in your money in the account for a specified time period. With money market deposit accounts, on the other hand, you will be required to maintain a higher minimum balance (normally $1,000) in your account.

Create Your Emergency Fund

None of us can really foresee the future. Therefore, it is always important to set up an emergency fund for times of crisis. This emergency fund is actually different from your general savings, so you need to keep them in separate accounts. Maintaining separate accounts will minimize your temptation to use your emergency fund for your day-to-day expenses.

Having an adequate emergency fund can save you money during times of crisis, primarily because you will not be compelled to take out instant loans that charge high interest rates or cash in your long-term investments that can eliminate all your earnings or even a portion of your original investment.

Here are the steps in setting up your emergency fund:

1. Ideally, you should aim for an emergency fund that can cover your essential living expenses for a minimum of 3 months. The trick here is to first determine how much money you need to survive every month (rent, food, gas, utilities, among others) and then multiply it by 3 months. Then, set aside a specific amount every month for deposit to your emergency fund. You can start with just $20 to $50, until your total target amount is complete.

2. Deposit your emergency fund in an account that you can easily access during an emergency. A savings account and certain types of money market deposit accounts are ideal. Avoid keeping your emergency fund in long-term investment vehicles like stocks, mutual funds or CDs with long maturity dates.

3. Make sure that you will only use your emergency fund for genuine emergency expenses, like unforeseen medical bills or unpredicted unemployment. Buying new clothes is not an emergency!

Chapter 5: Plan For Your Future

No matter what your current financial situation is, you always have to believe that you deserve an abundant and happy life. I hope that the previous two chapters have helped you better understand your addiction to shopping, how you can pay off your debts and how you can start saving. But now you may be asking, what for? Perhaps you have heard people say that money cannot really buy everything. Money cannot buy happiness. Money cannot buy love and friendship. Money cannot buy a good reputation. Those are all true. But if you think about it, a lot of your dreams in life actually require money. And this is what you need to ask yourself. What are my dreams in life? Only after you have answered this question will you be able to start setting goals and take the necessary actions to achieve them.

What are your financial goals?

Do you know that there are a lot of people who have never actually asked themselves about what they would like to achieve in their lives? Many people are very busy just trying to get through day-to-day living. Their focus is on promptly paying their bills, taking care of the household and taking care of their families. But if you ask them if they feel happy and fulfilled with their lives, if they feel in control of their own destiny and if they feel that they are fulfilling their hearts' desires, many of them will say, "No." One of the main reasons is that they failed to plan. You need to plan in order to have full control of your life. And the first step in successful planning is goal setting.

Your financial goals are those things that you wish to achieve in life that require money. An example could be: "I want to purchase a $1,000 computer by the end of this year" or "I want to save $300 per month for the coming year for a nice vacation with my wife." If you look at these examples, you will note that they include a time frame (end of this year and coming year) and dollar amounts ($1,000 and $300 per month). These two examples are considered SMART because they are Specific, Measurable, Achievable, Realistic and Time-bound.

It is possible for you to have various financial goals that have varying time frames. Typically, you could divide your financial goals into 3 time frames: short-term, medium term and long-term. Short-term goals are those you want to achieve within the next 3 months. For instance, you want to buy a new smartphone within the next 3 months. Medium-term goals are those you want to achieve within 3 to 12 months. For instance, you want to purchase a new oven within 6 months. Lastly, long-term goals are those you want to achieve within 1 year or more. For instance, you want to save $10,000 for the down payment on a new house.

After you are done with your goal setting, the next step is to determine how much you need to save every week or every month to achieve your goals. You will also need to be able to track your progress. But before you start with your computations, it is ideal for you to determine your needs and wants that require money. You can start by simply writing down whatever comes to your mind. After you have brainstormed, you can then prioritize your "wishes" by determining which ones are the most important goals for you. Then you can assign a time frame for each goal that you want to prioritize.

Financial Goals You May Want to Think About

Goal setting is a personal thing. There are really no right and wrong answers. What may be important to you may not be important to other people. The right answer depends on what you truly need and desire. However, it is important for you to involve your spouse and family in setting your goals since most of your goals will also affect them.

Here are some financial goals that you may want to consider:

- Short-term goals: settle your credit card debts, set up your emergency fund, enhance your computer system, purchase a new wardrobe, purchase furniture and equipment for your home

- Medium-term goals: enrol in a new class or training, start setting up your investments, start giving more to your favorite charities, go on a dream vacation, purchase either a used or new car, enhance your emergency fund

- Long-term goals: purchase a new house, save for your children's education, set up your own business, save for your retirement, purchase investment properties (e.g. apartments for rent)

After you are done with your goal setting and you already know how much money you have to save every month to achieve your goals, you are now ready to proceed to achieving them. Remember what we discussed in the previous chapter, you need to pay yourself first. If ever a crisis or emergency happens, do not be discouraged if you have to make slight changes in your plan. Simply re-commit to begin saving again as soon as possible.

A Budget Is Your Most Effective Tool

After you have determined what you want to achieve in life, it is now time for you make things happen. It is but natural for you to feel scared that you do not have the money to meet all of your financial goals. But do not worry. Research studies have shown that an average American family squanders 30% of their income ($0.30 for every $1.00) because of wasteful spending habits. Avoid those wasteful habits can actually be compared to earning an additional 30% of income. To do this, you need to create your budget.

A budget is basically a tool that will allow you to take control of your finances and your life. It is the most effective tool you can use to achieve your financial goals. Below are the steps to creating your budget. But you need to always remember that for your budget to be an effective tool, you need to practice accuracy in making it. You need to spend time recording and calculating your income and expenses. Do not compute inside your head, use pen, paper and calculator or better, use the computer. As much as possible, avoid using estimates.

Step 1: Determine your household income.

One thing you should definitely avoid is overestimating your income. This will not really help you in the long run. Be accurate but extensive in identifying your income. Some of the things you may include are: salaries and wages (after taxes), job bonuses, tips and overtime pay (guaranteed or best estimate), interest income from savings and investment accounts (guaranteed or best estimate), social security benefits, child support, tax refund, pension benefits, business income, rental income and gifts.

Step 2: List Down your Living Expenses

You can use your credit card or checking account statements for the previous 3 months to help you determine the average amounts you spend on your living expenses. Some of the expenses you may include in your list are: savings and investments (remember, pay yourself first), rent or home mortgage, utilities (electricity, water, gas/heating oil, telephone, cell phone, cable TV, internet), food and groceries, dining out, transportation (car loan payments, gasoline, car repair and maintenance, insurance premium, public transportation), child care, child support, spousal maintenance or child care, medical/dental bills, insurance premiums (health, life, homeowner's, property, renter's), pet care, property tax, professional association or union dues, clothing, donations, other loan payments (including credit cards), personal expenses, home repair, maintenance and improvement.

Step 3: Compare your total monthly income against your total monthly expenses.

When your monthly income is higher than your monthly expenses, it means that you can set aside more money to achieve your financial goals. On the other hand, if your monthly expenses are higher than your monthly income, it means that you need to take immediate actions to either increase your income or decrease your expenses so you achieve your financial goals.

Step 4: Take action by setting priorities and making necessary changes.

This step is critical if you have a negative cash flow (monthly expenses greater than monthly income). This situation can actually happen to anyone of us, no matter what income level we might have. Do not panic. The good news is that you are now aware of your situation and therefore, you can take the appropriate actions to give you control over your finances and your life again.

The ideal step that you can take is to increase your household income while you decrease your household expenses. Here are some options you can take to increase your income: find a higher paying

Shopping Addiction Therapy

job that you like, talk to your boss if you can work overtime, see if your schedule will allow you to take another job, consider earning money from your hobbies, sell your possession that you rarely use.

To decrease your expenses, review the list of expenses that you have just created and see which ones you can cut back on. Refer to the list of tips in Chapter 3 on how you can reduce your monthly expenses.

Enjoy the Adventure and the Journey

Taking control of your finances and your life is not an easy task. But those who take on the challenge are rewarded tremendously. You just need to always remind yourself that you deserve an abundant life, no matter what your situation is right now. The lessons you have just learned are only tools that can help you restore your life and achieve your life dreams. But your success greatly depends on you. You also need to realize that you cannot make this journey on your own. You need to reach out to your family and friends who can make your journey more fruitful and exciting. If you find yourself slipping back into your old habits or your shopping addiction, review what you have just learned and get right back on your feet!

Conclusion

Thank you again for purchasing this book!

I hope this book was able to help you to have a better understanding of shopping addiction and how you can recover from it.

The next step is to apply the techniques and strategies that you have just learned. Always keep in mind that money is not your life. What truly matters is what you are doing with money to achieve your dreams in life.

Thank you and good luck!